Claire Zimmerman

MIES VAN DER ROHE

1886–1969

The Structure of Space

TASCHEN

HONG KONG KÖLN LONDON LOS ANGELES MADRID PARIS TOKYO

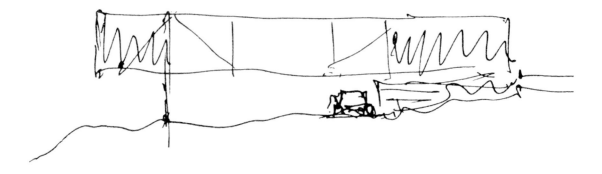

Illustration page 2 ▶ Ludwig Mies van der Rohe at
Crown Hall in 1956
Illustration above ▶ Glass house on a hillside.
Sketch, c. 1934

© 2006 TASCHEN GmbH
Hohenzollernring 53, D-50672 Köln
www.taschen.com

Editor ▶ Peter Gössel, Bremen
Design and layout ▶ Gössel und Partner, Bremen
Project management ▶ Swantje Schmidt, Bremen
Text edited by ▶ Johannes Althoff, Berlin

Printed in Germany
ISBN 978-3-8228-3643-9

To stay informed about upcoming TASCHEN
titles, please request our magazine at
www.taschen.com/magazine or write to
TASCHEN America, 6671 Sunset Boulevard,
Suite 1508, USA-Los Angeles, CA 90028,
contact-us@taschen.com, Fax: +1-323-463.4442.
We will be happy to send you a free copy of our
magazine which is filled with information about
all of our books.

Contents

Introduction

Ludwig Mies van der Rohe was not fond of frequent public pronouncement. Nevertheless, he left behind a substantial body of works, both constructed and unbuilt, from which a modern theory of architecture emerges with particular, organic clarity. His published statements were few and eminently well reasoned. His buildings, equally, are well thought-out, clearly formulated responses to the architectural challenges of the 20th century. His output, particularly over the second half of his career, gives evidence of a carefully considered, highly evolved set of solutions for repeated use. And while the quality of his work was almost uniformly high, his greatest influence may arguably be traced to the types or archetypes he developed in the post-WWII years. Mies's own high-rise buildings are numerous, but their imitators and clones are much more so, and occasionally threaten to overwhelm them. Similarly, Mies's pavilions grace a number of important sites in cities on two continents, whereas their followers are spread across office parks and ex-urban landscapes over a wider terrain.

Mies' career was definitively shaped by events of the 20th century. He occupied one position in German architecture culture until the late 1930s, and quite a different one across the ocean in Chicago after 1938. A maverick talent from a provincial town far from the cosmopolitan center of Berlin, he made his mark through ability and strength of character, without the aid of wealth or an elite education. In contrast, from the moment he arrived in Chicago, Mies was an eminence *gris* with a reputation as one of Europe's most talented modern architects, and an expert on progressive European culture. Throughout his long life, however, he remained absorbed in a single task; finding solutions to the new architectural problems of an industrialized age.

Mies arrived in Berlin in 1905 at the age of 19. The son of a stonemason, he had attended the Cathedral School in Aachen, which he left in 1899 without qualification. After attending local trade school, he became an apprentice on building sites and developed his skills in freehand sketching at a company that specialized in decorative plasterwork. By the time he arrived in Berlin, Mies could draft at full scale on a vertical drawing board, lay bricks and carve stone. The tasks of design and construction were combined in his early education, not separated by increasingly common divisions between architect and builder. The medieval fabric of his hometown, Aachen, further undermined traditional divisions between architecture and craft, thanks to well-constructed architecture built over more than a millennium in the old imperial seat of Charlemagne, with its 8th century cathedral and its direct historical connection to the traditions of antiquity. Mies would have come away from Aachen with the fundamental belief in an architecture of the *longue durée*, where building form signified a lasting symbolic function, not a short-term programmatic one.

Mies's education continued in a different vein in the German imperial capital. While working as a draftsman for architect Bruno Paul, he studied from 1906 until 1908, both at the *Kunstgewerbeschule* (School for Arts and Crafts) and at the *Hochschule für bildende Künste* (School of Fine Arts). Turn of the century Berlin was in the midst of an artistic awakening triggered by the new century, by developments in France and Eng-

land, and by the influence of Friedrich Nietzsche. Progressive artists and intellectuals gradually worked to cast off historical precedent in favor of 'the new,' often seen to lie in the aestheticizing of everyday life. The attempt to absorb history within a new language of form challenged members of the Reform movements, organized since 1907 in the *German Werkbund*, in a variety of disciplines. It had, however, a particular urgency in architecture, which brought modernity to the denizens of the city in a notably public way.

Mies was only 20 when he received his first independent commission in 1906. This was a house for philosophy professor Alois Riehl and his wife Sophie in the Potsdam suburb of Neubabelsberg. In the course of the project Mies became friends with Riehl, one of the leading Nietzsche experts of the time, who opened up a new world for the young architect. Soon a regular guest of the Riehl family, Mies met representatives of the Berlin intelligentsia at their house. Among these industrialist, writer and politician Walther Rathenau, philosopher Eduard Spranger, and eminent art-historian Heinrich Wölfflin, a theoretical father of modernism, stand out. There Mies also met Ada Bruhn, at the time Wölfflin's fiancée, but destined to marry Mies in 1913.

The success of the commission, completed in 1907, paved the way for Mies's 1908 entry into the atelier of Peter Behrens, at that time one of the most important architectural offices in Europe. The year before, Behrens was appointed by the Allgemeine Elektrizitäts Gesellschaft (AEG) to the artistic advisory board and commissioned with the creation of a uniform industry-design. The aim of the design was the creation of a corporate identity for the Berlin electricity conglomerate, in the sense of a total artwork, which included the designing of industrial buildings. Mies claimed that Behrens taught him the significance of "the Great Form," evident in buildings such as Behrens's Turbine Hall of 1909. Furthermore, it was under Behrens's tutelage that Mies encountered the work of Karl Friedrich Schinkel, an important lifelong influence on his work. Mies's interest in Schinkel's clear language of form is manifested perhaps most clearly in his Perls House of 1911, in Berlin-Zehlendorf.

Mies in front of Riehl House, Potsdam-Neubabelsberg, c. 1910

At this time Mies was first exposed to the work of Frank Lloyd Wright, possibly at a lecture in 1910 in Berlin, but more likely in Wright's 1911 Wasmuth monograph folio. "Here," Mies later remembered, "finally, was a master-builder drawing upon the veritable fountainhead of architecture." Another important influence on Mies would become apparent in the 1920's, when Mies analyzed the writings of the Dutch architect Hendrik Petrus Berlage. Whereas Behrens, a follower of Nietzsche and Riegl, understood art as an image of the will, of the "will to style," as he called it, Berlage, as a follower of Plato and Hegel, in addition to Viollet-le-Duc and Semper, viewed architecture as an organic process of rational discovery: a search for the absolutely rational as an essential truth. Analogous to nature, the art of architecture was to discover new prototypes and new organic structures. Behrens saw the architect as a demiurge, whose destiny was the creation of a new form, someone who was "form-giving." For Berlage, the task of an architect was a constructive "form-finding:" "Building is serving." Mies himself stated that it was Berlage who imparted to him the "idea of clear construction as one of the fundamentals we should accept." "Behrens taught me the Great Form, Berlage the structure," Mies admitted in his later years. Indeed, this claim illuminates his later practice and is reflected in his New National Gallery in Berlin, Crown Hall and the unbuilt Convention Hall in Chicago. They might all be related to Behrens's archetypal industrial buildings. However, in their visibility of structure and basic shapes they are committed to Berlage's approach.

Mies established his own business in Berlin in 1912. He was aided in this by his 1913 marriage to Ada Bruhn. As the daughter of a well-to-do manufacturer, Ada had a small personal fortune that buffered the Mies family from financial insecurity in the early years of Mies's practice. As he pursued connections within Berlin artistic circles, Mies continued building private houses for well-to-do clients, mostly in the nobler Berlin and Potsdam suburbs. These buildings often followed a neo-classical style and showed that Mies was evidently aware of debates in the pre-World War I Reform movements, and influenced by figures such as Hermann Muthesius and Karl Scheffler. However, it was not until after World War I, in which Mies served from 1915–1918, that he began to develop a new language of architecture.

Revolutionary Berlin, to which Mies returned after the war, was engulfed by radical changes in the political as well as artistic arenas. In the 1920s the city became one of the centers of the European avant-garde, where an increasingly international artistic scene aimed to create a new society and a new citizen in this society. Against this pro-

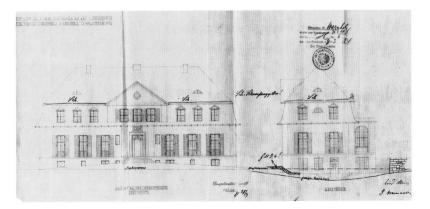

Warnholtz House, Heerstrasse, Berlin-Charlottenburg, 1914–1915
Elevation drawing from recently discovered permit set

Cover of G (no. 3, June 1924), with elevation drawing of Mies's Glass Skyscraper Project of 1922

gressively more radical backdrop, Mies' unsuccessful submission to Walter Gropius's 1919 Exhibition of Unknown Architects was a critical experience in the young architect's career. Mies took the rejection of his submitted Kröller-Müller Villa Project (1912–1913) to heart: Gropius apparently criticized its lack of modernity.

Although he continued to build within established conventions, Mies increasingly concerned himself with theoretical questions on the nature of architecture, tackling an experimental field of work. He participated in the discourse of the avant-garde and joined the November group, an association of radical artists. He also joined his friend Hans Richter, artist and filmmaker, in editing and publishing the avant-garde journal G Zeitschrift für elementare Gestaltung. Members of the expanded G-circle included Hans Arp, Walter Benjamin, Ludwig Hilberseimer, Theo van Doesburg, Naum Gabo, El Lissitzky, George Grosz and Man Ray. In 1924, Mies was invited to join the German Werkbund, one of the most powerful organizations of modern German culture.

In 1921 Mies effectively dissolved his marriage, although he and Ada Mies never divorced. He also changed his name to "Mies van der Rohe", countering the negative associations of the German mies ("miserable" or "rotten" in English). Adding the compound "van der Rohe" signified, on the one hand, an adaptation of his mother's maiden name, "Rohe," and on the other, the German word "roh," understood as "pure" or "unadulterated." This addition might also point to the elementary form of building and construction that Mies at that time strived for. Like numerous other European intellectuals such as Arthur Moeller van den Bruck and Le Corbusier, Mies created his own public persona through self-naming.

Between 1921 and 1924 Mies designed five projects, none of which were realized. Posterity has remembered them as the famous "Five Projects." Indeed, these five conceptual exercises catapulted Mies to the top rank of the avant-garde. The first, a glass skyscraper for a building site at Friedrichstrasse in Berlin-Mitte, was one of the most radical projects of his entire career. A submission to the first major skyscraper competition in the city, which challenged German architects to adapt and transform this new building type, the project also partook of a wave of Americanism. Four of the "Five Projects" ere published in G in the early 1920s. The idea of clear construction as a precondition of building is revealed here: "The materials are concrete, iron, glass," Mies explained. "Ferroconcrete buildings are essentially skeleton structures. Neither pastry nor tank turrets. ... That means skin and bone structures." In accordance with this insight the rejection of form-finding à la Behrens equally implied the rejection of established building methods in favor of a way of building that followed an organic logic. At the time, Mies addressed one of the five projects thus: "We know no forms, only building problems. Form is not the goal but the result of our work. There is no form in and for itself. ... Form as goal is formalism; and that we reject. Nor do we strive for a style. ... It is our specific concern to liberate building activity from aesthetic speculators and make building again what alone it should be, namely BUILDING."

For Mies, contemporary building meant modern materials and modern building techniques aggregated in an architecture appropriate to contemporary society. In the early 1920s he reduced these considerations to a simple formula: "The building art is the spatially apprehended will of the epoch. Alive. Changing. New." It was necessary to determine, beyond any aesthetic speculation, an essential idea of building-form that reflected an absolutely determined idea of the nature of architecture. Dematerialization of a fixed body, due to radical reduction of the buildings to "skin and bone"

buildings, revealed as its innermost core the inner order of the construction; and the inner order resulted in structure. Mies' understanding of the term structure he later explained as follows: "By structure we (Europeans) have a philosophical idea. The structure is the whole, from top to bottom, to the last detail-with the same ideas. That is what we call 'structure'." Along these lines Mies demanded in 1923 a new attitude towards building characterized by "absolute truthfulness and rejection of all formal cheating." This did not mean, however, an embrace of structural rationalism as the equivalent of constructed truth. In this sense, Mies's 'structure' is also always a conceptual structure, whose realization in construction can be achieved through a variety of means. He would remain true to this practice for the rest of his life. Mies' distancing from the Behrens´ position became more and more apparent in the early 1920s. In 1928 he would express it in a note, referring to Behrens' Turbine Hall: "The nature of the technical is determined in its fulfilment. ... He who builds a factory as if it were a temple lies and disfigures the landscape."

The year 1926 marked a turning point in Mies' biography. At the age of 40 he assumed vice presidency of the *German Werkbund*, a position he would hold until 1932. He was thus well positioned as a central figure in German architecture and in the fledgling movement for international modernism then blossoming among intellectuals in France, Germany, the Netherlands and Belgium. At the same time, he was commissioned to direct "The Dwelling," a major *Werkbund* exhibition slated to take place in the city of Stuttgart in 1927. The exhibition marked his first collaboration with Lilly Reich, who would be his companion and collaborator till 1938. With material exhibits in the city center, and the critically important housing settlement called the *Weissenhofsiedlung*, the exhibition served as a demonstration of the work of *Neues Bauen*, the group of modernists of whom Mies formed an essential member. A full-scale architecture and construction laboratory, it included an international roster of participating architects testing new ideas for design and construction. Many of them investigated prototypes for industrialized architecture; Mies, by contrast, hoped to

Interior view of the exhibition house at the Berlin Building Exhibition, "The Dwelling of our Time," 1931

Mies teaching at the *Bauhaus*, ca. 1931

refine the technical possibilities of *Neues Bauen* in accord with his own search for architectural value.

Mies himself called the year 1926 "the most significant" one in his career. Indeed, it was the year when Mies broke new ground in the handling of space, distancing himself from his strictly materialist position of the early 1920s in favor of an idealistic one that inevitably returned to formal and aesthetic questions. The problem of *Neues Bauen* was for Mies not any longer just a "question of materials" but "basically a spiritual problem" that "can only be solved by creative forces," in which the question of living became an "element of the larger struggle for new forms of living." In this regard, he achieved significant results at the Stuttgart exhibition: his apartment block at the *Weissenhofsiedlung*, with a load-bearing steel frame construction, contained apartments with nonstructural partition walls, which produced potentially flexible ground plans. With his famous Glass Room at the Materials show in Stuttgart's inner city, Mies discovered a new design system critical to his future work— a compositional system that produced an open ground-plan with fluid transitions between spaces and an implied sense of spatial choreography.

An important influence on Mies's development after *Weissenhof* were the writings of the religious philosopher Romano Guardini and the work of the Guardini-influenced architect Rudolf Schwarz. Guardini's dialectic philosophy enabled Mies to overcome conflicts between the inconsistency of order and freedom, nature and form. In the end, Guardini's philosophical innovations were founded on connecting the Platonic-Hegelian idea to what would come to be known as modern existential philosophy. Supplementary to structure—as the nature-reflecting element of building—Mies now returned to form as an expression of the artist's will and as the evident physical presence of constructed architecture.

The new experience of space discovered in the Glass Room was first exhibited in developed form in the 1929 German Pavilion in Barcelona and at the Villa Tugendhat, built in 1930 in Brno. These groundbreaking buildings brought Mies international

attention; in them a radically new notion of dynamic space emerged. Here space was conceived in close association with movement, so that particular spatial experiences, through space and time, result. Mies's ground plans now begin to read as choreographical devices that encode the sequence of contrasting experiences that is their most powerful attribute. With these projects Mies entered into an arena of investigation that he would continue to explore under very different conditions for the rest of his life. His spatial experiments at Brno and Barcelona can be connected to the later investigations of the Farnsworth House, Crown Hall, and the New National Gallery, even while the differences between early and late projects is as dramatic as the continuity between them. Mies's engagement with space as a primary material of architecture answered a call from theoreticians that dates back to the 19th century; it represents the fulfillment of one of the most consistent demands for an architecture of the early 20th c.

The 1927 *Werkbund* exhibition had brought the cultural radicalism of Berlin to conservative Stuttgart. The local architectural community criticized the project, from which they had been largely excluded. Whereas progressive architects considered the *Weissenhofsiedlung* a resounding success, architects of a different political persuasion disagreed, seeing the power of modernists within the *Werkbund* as a threat to German culture and traditions. Criticism of *Neues Bauen* increased after 1927, first having material effect after the financial crisis of 1929, and resulting in decreasing commissions for *Neues Bauen* architects in the early years of the 1930s.

The years immediately following the Stuttgart exhibition were among Mies's most productive, and influenced future generations substantially. In recognition of his increasingly centrist role in German cultural politics, Mies was offered the directorship of the troubled Dessau *Bauhaus* in 1930. The unofficial educational arm of *Neues Bauen* and of progressive art in other media, the *Bauhaus* was threatened with closure in 1930. Mies took the chair from Swiss architect Hannes Meyer, dismissed for transforming the school into a leftist political institution in a city whose local government was moving increasingly to the right. In 1931, after the NSDAP won the local elections,

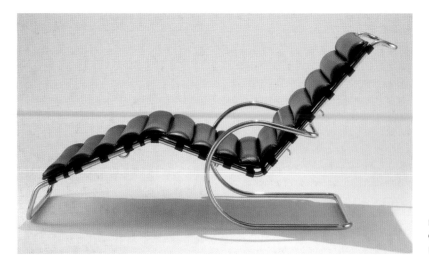

MR chaise longue with armrests, 1931–1932
Chromed steel tubes with leather cushions, Knoll
International

the new town council passed a resolution to close the school. Mies and his students
took refuge in an old factory building in Berlin-Steglitz. From there the *Bauhaus* continued to operate until it was voluntarily disbanded in 1933 as a result of the National
Socialist assumption of power.

By 1933, many architects of *Neues Bauen* understood their precarious status in
National Socialist Germany, and many emigrated. Mies remained until 1938, as more
and more restrictions were imposed on his work and his own security was threatened.
He first visited the United States in 1937 for a potential client. MoMA Trustee Helen
Resor knew his work from the 1932 International Style exhibition at the Museum of
Modern Art. But Mrs. Resor's interest in Mies, and indeed that of the whole American
culture scene, was almost single-handedly the work of MoMA curator Philip Johnson,
who had realized Mies's importance while curating his 1932 show with architectural
historian Henry Russell Hitchcock.

Returning to Germany briefly in 1938, Mies accepted the directorship of Chicago's
Armour Institute of Technology, later re-christened the Illinois Institute of Technology
(IIT). His appointment as head of the architecture department necessitated the design
of a curriculum and a newly enlarged campus. His transition to the United States was
thus smoothed by the security of an academic post and the offer of large building commissions, then so completely lacking in Germany for an architect like Mies.

Mies's work in the United States changed radically, although related themes re-
emerged over time. Firstly, he designed only two private houses of lasting significance,
and only one of those under commission from a client. Secondly, an entire campus of
predominantly low-rise buildings for IIT brought the issue of type-solutions and modular design to the center of his concerns. Thirdly, technological advances to the building
industry after World War II, combined with an increased volume of commissions com-
ing into Mies's office, resulted in steel construction on an unprecedented scale. In addition, increased commissions for high-rise buildings returned the architect to themes
that had occupied him exclusively on paper in his German years, in a series of unbuilt
skyscraper designs from 1921–1929. In America, these schematic, abstract notations
were finally turned into solid objects. Details studied intensively by Mies in these years
included steel-to-steel, steel-to-brick, and steel-to-glass connections.

Mies's increased project load also necessitated a shift in scale. From the mid-sized building worked as a highly crafted discrete object, Mies came to work increasingly on the urban master plan and the repeated, industrially produced construction detail. Symptomatically, he produced no new furniture designs, abandoning an important business outlet that had helped sustain him in Germany.

Mies earlier conceptual interests were also transformed by new working conditions. Whereas his German clients were generally private individuals and public constellations (the *German Werkbund*, the German government, the Union of Plate Glass Manufacturers), institutional and corporate clients in the United States demanded less art and more repeatability. Even in his residential projects, Mies generally worked with the developer, not with potential residents. This resulted in an increased emphasis on flexibility of use over time. In this way Mies began to develop the architectural archetypes of modern capitalism.

The American context also altered Mies's public persona. Formerly one of a group of progressive-minded architects, of whom he was by no means the best-known or most successful, Mies became an almost instant celebrity in Chicago's cultural circles. From his directorship of IIT to his congenial collaboration with the enlightened developer Herbert Greenwald, Mies's activities placed him in a position of social and cultural importance. This new stature carried an increased latitude in the further development of his own architectural interests within the constraints of profitability. In contrast to his German years, and to the later evacuation of structure from the interior of his large spaces, Mies developed a system where building skin and frame were once again connected to each other, in his buildings for IIT. Furthermore, he developed an integrated system of modules as determinants of architectural space. The 22 buildings Mies designed and built there, show the advantages of a system that allowed a large degree of similitude in architectural solutions with an equal flexibility to accommodate difference.

The challenge of modular design and construction also occupied Mies's attention in the many high-rise buildings of his American years. IIT demanded a flexible design system that could spread horizontally (based on a 24-foot module); the high-rise designs required a carefully detailed building skin. This problem of the vertical, rather than the horizontal plane, involved far more sophisticated engineering solutions. In addition, codes demanding fire retardant for steel structure over one story high introduced an extra layer between the building's structure and its exterior skin. Mies first confronted this new condition in two-story buildings for IIT, devising some of his most brilliant and best-known solutions, in response to it. The load-bearing structure is echoed in non-structural steel elements on the building's skin, depicting the encased steelwork frame on the façade and at the corners of the building. Thus Mies's earlier ideas of the importance of a clear conceptual structure emerged in his IIT work with a diagrammatic clarity. In the high-rise buildings, the problem of internal skeleton versus external expression became even more focused. Mies's efforts to show the internal structures of his tall buildings on their exterior skins evolved into representing an *idea* of clear structure. He had sheathed his Barcelona columns in cruciform chrome wrappers, creating a conceptual structure over the engineered structure to give it a different meaning. In the American skyscrapers, conceptual structures depicted on articulated curtain walls also presented the complex engineering of his high-rise designs as Mies wished them to be understood. This was a process that developed over a period of

Mies with the developer Herbert Greenwald, c. 1955

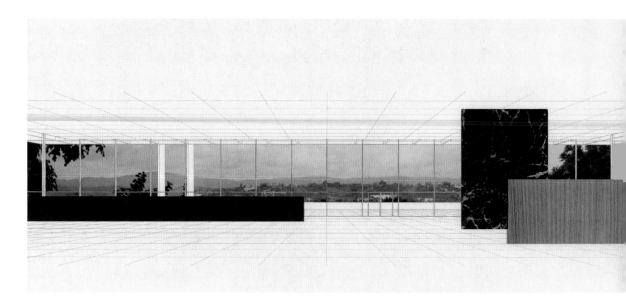

Bacardí Office Building Project for Santiago, Cuba, 1957
Interior view with photo collage

years. Slowly, his task had become clearer: to make buildings carry an idea about them selves that was not dependent on literal 'truth,' but rather on a clear structural idea.

As much as Mies's living and working conditions might have changed after his move to the United States, and as much as he was now confronted with entirely differ ent architectural challenges, continuities with his earlier years also emerge with impo tance. In particular, the type solutions—the archetypes—he developed at this tim took up his search for a new language of architectural form and recall his contribution to public intellectual discourse in Germany. These late projects recall Mies's earlies statements about the essential qualities of a modern architecture, and deliver on th promises made in the 1920s. That early theo-retical decisions could only be imple mented late in Mies's career is not surprising; but it reinforces the notable persistenc between early and late modernism, between pre-war European, and post-war America contexts. The Seagram Building was undoubt-edly designed in this paradigmat fashion. It is often seen as the finest high-rise building Mies ever built. No longer look ing back to past historical style for legitimation, the building presents the architectur of capitalism with its most essential, concentrated face. Simultaneously, it suggest the importance of the public sphere through its location on Park Avenue.

A group of conceptual projects executed over a broad span of years make a interesting comparison with his famous "Five Projects" of the early 1920s. As he ha done in Germany, Mies used these projects (mostly executed with IIT students) to tes out new ideas. These theoretical works share a common constructional theme: th separation of the roof and its supports from the spatial events found beneath. In all bu the first the sheltering roof of the building was autonomous from the interior, as fre from internal columns as possible. The creation of a support-free space constituted significant engineering challenge, but we might also note the philosophical implica tions of this process, which occupied so much of Mies's attention. Resuming his ea lier investigations of 'free planning' (with reference to the works of Guardini), and i particular the idea of the large empty space as the meeting place of human being an nature—Mies pursued a space for any program activity, with complete freedom fror

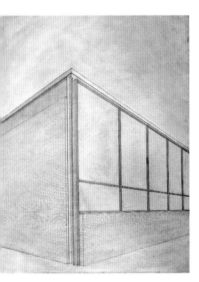

Library and Administration Building Project,
Illinois Institute of Technology
Perspective of corner detail, 1944–1945
Delineator: Sing Mau Chau

structural constraint. Mies created these one-room-buildings, beyond mundane purpose or clear programmed activity, with complete freedom from structural constraint. We might contrast this idea of the empty space, increasingly more urgent as the years went by, with the very different task of the IIT campus that had confronted him upon his arrival in 1938. But we might also note the overall design strategy, the development of an archetypal spatial organization that is both repeatable and usable for a wide variety of individual purposes.

Open plan buildings now became the focus of Mies's attention. The two-way structure of his experimental 50 x 50 House (1951) opened a rich vein that Mies worked for many years, culminating in the great pavilion museum in the partially destroyed city of his professional youth. Significant program functions (art display, offices, workrooms, retail spaces, bathrooms) occupied the basement of the New National Gallery in Berlin. The vast pavilion of the entry level is best left nearly empty. As Mies himself noted in a film by his daughter Georgia, "It is such a huge hall that of course it means great difficulties for the exhibiting of art. I am fully aware of that. But it has such potential that I simply cannot take those difficulties into account." Perhaps Mies was embracing Adolf Loos's claim that architecture resides only in the monument and the tomb. Or perhaps he had just determined that architecture need not solve all problems associated with daily use, particularly if it attended to a different understanding of architectural function, at once richly sensual and cerebrally platonic.

1906–1907 ▸ Riehl House

Spitzweggasse 3, Potsdam-Neubabelsberg, Germany

View from the lower garden
Left page: Contemporary photograph
Left: Picture about 1910

Right:
View across rose garden toward house entry

Mies's obtained his first building commission on the recommendation of a fellow-worker in the office of Bruno Paul. Berlin philosophy professor Alois Riehl and his wife Sophie planned a weekend house in the elegant suburb of Neubabelsberg. In an interview with his grandson in the 1960s, Mies claimed to have rejected Paul's offers of help on this challenging commission point blank. He also noted that the Riehls wished to engage an eager young talent rather than an established professional, and that Sophie Riehl had sent him to Italy in company with a colleague from the Paul office, "to become more mature" in preparation for the commission.

The house followed the prevailing taste for a simple, pragmatic style with references to late 18th / early 19th century domestic architecture as well as to the English Arts and Crafts Movement. The interior is organized around a central hall paneled in a thin gridded lattice reminiscent of contemporary interiors by Paul, but also recalling the work of Richard Riemerschmid. Service spaces occupy the basement below, and bedrooms are located on the floor above. Mies paid close attention to new developments in garden design, initiated by Hermann Muthesius, that advocated the 'architectonic garden' as an important means to integrate house and site. Here, he designed discrete garden spaces for different purposes: the rose garden on the entry side of the house, with closed borders and geometrical planting beds; the smaller and more secluded garden walk alongside Riehl's study; the large, less ordered landscape below the retaining wall that divides the house from its dramatic slope, with tree plantings, winding paths, and a small tea pavilion (now destroyed). The house obtains its greatest dramatic effect from the view of the Griebnitzsee revealed from the loggia that overlooks the garden on the ground floor (now glazed in).

With this early commission, the young Mies proved himself able to design and build competently, even skillfully, and capable of productively engaging the most contemporary issues of the architectural world in Berlin at the time. Anton Jaumann called the work, "so faultless that one would never guess it is a young architect's first independent work." Mies was twenty-one when the Riehl House was completed in 1907.

Main floor plan

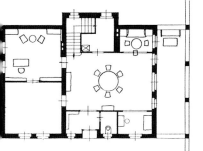

1910 ▸ Bismarck Monument
Not realized ▸ Bingen on Rhine, Germany

View of interior court, with statue of Bismarck
Gouache on linen rendering rediscovered in late 1990s

Photo collage of site with model of Mies brothers' design

The Bismarck Monument Competition was a large national competition intended to commemorate the 1915 centennial of the great German statesman Otto von Bismarck. The project was to be sited on the banks of the river Rhine, near Bingen. Taking a leave from his work with Peter Behrens, Mies returned home to Aachen and prepared the design over several months. He entered the competition with his brother Ewald, who was to execute the statue of Bismarck. The competition drew numerous entries. In a disputed decision the jury, which included well-known figures like Max Dessoir, Walther Rathenau, and Hermann Muthesius, favored the joint design of architect German Bestelmeyer and sculptor Hermann Hahn. Ludwig and Ewald Mies's entry received special merit, but no prize. The jury admired the design. But it criticized the impracticality of the project's enormous podium, to be built out over the steep river valley site.

The design consists of two lateral colonnaded wings terminating in large rectangular masses that anchor the composition to its podium. A statue of Bismarck was to occupy an apsidal columned hall between these. The building style echoes the severely classical work of Peter Behrens and of Karl Friedrich Schinkel before him, but also recalls the work of other German architects like Alfred Messel.

1912–1913 ▸ Kröller-Müller Villa
Not realized ▸ Wassenaar, Netherlands

Perspective sketch in watercolor and pastel, showing pergola and large gallery

After Mies returned to Peter Behrens's office in 1911, he was sent east to supervise construction of the German Embassy in St. Petersburg, and then west to develop Behrens's design for a villa and art museum in the Netherlands. Commissioned by the wealthy industrialist A.G. Kröller and his art-collector wife Helene, Behrens's design was ultimately rejected, and the couple then asked the young Mies to prepare an alternative scheme of his own. At the same time, they asked the Dutch architect Hendrik Petrus Berlage to do the same, thus putting Mies in competition with one of the most eminent architects of the day. Neither design was constructed, although Berlage's was deemed more successful at the time.

Mies's scheme (which led to his final departure from Behrens's office) includes a series of distinct flat-roofed building volumes assembled to create enclosed and semi-enclosed garden spaces flanked by long galleries and colonnades. The main wing of the villa is a two-storied rectangular volume set back between side wings on the entry front, and annexed to three other volumes forming an enclosed court on the garden side. Further garden planning is most clear in the surviving model photographs, which show a sequence of outdoor terraces and sunken gardens that integrate the building with its landscape site. The house records Mies's earliest encounters with the work of contemporary and historical forerunners: with Frank Lloyd Wright (whose work was published in Germany in 1910/1911); with the great Schinkel, whose work Mies studied closely while working for Behrens; and with Behrens himself.

1921–1924 · The "Five Projects"

All projects not realized ▸ Friedrichstrasse Skyscraper, Glass Skyscraper, Concrete Office Building, Concrete Country House, Brick Country House

Between 1921 and 1924 Mies executed his now-famous "Five Projects," so grouped by historians and critics as if to constitute a deliberate manifesto. In fact the five-project grouping is a creation of modern scholarship. In two skyscraper prototypes, two country villas, and one office building design, Mies addressed some of the pressing issues confronting *Neues Bauen* in Germany, and simultaneously developed architectural interests that would resonate in his practice for decades.

The first skyscraper design was dubbed "Wabe" (honeycomb) by Mies in a nod to the cellular construction of the tall office building. Also known as the Friedrichstrasse Skyscraper, the project was executed for the triangular patch of land bounded by the Friedrichstrasse train station, the Friedrichstrasse, and the Spree River in Berlin in 1921. Mies' concept was that of a steel framework with cantilevered floors clad in glass. He rejected the usual architectural style of American skyscrapers at the time, in which steel was clad in brick or terracotta, preferring to show each floor level on the building skin. The project thus made visible the principle of its construction. The complex angled structure of the building as well as its geometrically complex footprint resulted partly from the shape of the available site; but it probably also stemmed from the architect's ongoing investigation of the reflective properties of plate glass, openly acknowledged in his next skyscraper design. The building would have appeared as if striped by variegated light striking its many vertical surfaces; its structural transparency was thus

Friedrichstrasse Skyscraper project, 1921
Typical floor plan

Left page:
Friedrichstrasse Skyscraper Project, 1921
Perspective view from north, in charcoal and pencil

Glass Skyscraper Project, 1922
Typical floor plan

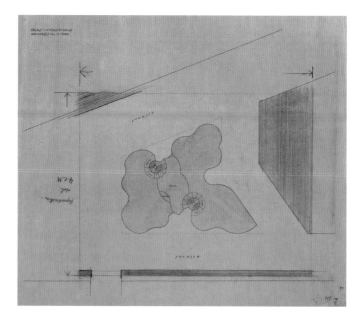

Glass Skyscraper Project, 1922
View of glass model in site model

Concrete Office Building Project, 1923
Perspective view in charcoal and crayon

counteracted and offset in nearly dialectical fashion by this simultaneous opacity. Mies was also no doubt influenced by the Expressionist movement unfolding after the First World War, and its advocacy of crystalline form. Finally, his own interests were moving toward a search for organic building design, a search that would occupy him for the rest of his professional life. An important clue to the building's structural concept can be found in a photograph of the elevation drawing that was later cut down: just visible along the edge of the original drawing sheet (now lost) are a couple of small flower sketches. Mies apparently believed that the building's floor slabs might be cantilevered off a central 'stalk'.

The second skyscraper (The Glass Skyscraper, 1922) was designed for an unknown Berlin site in 1922. It traded the crystalline geometries of the Friedrichstrasse design for biomorphic, curvilinear form. It was based on the idea of concrete slabs cantilevered off concrete columns distributed throughout the interior. The design would probably have proved impossible to construct at the time. The particular shape of the footprint derived from the shape of the site, and again from the transparent/reflective properties of its glass skin, this time openly acknowledged by the architect, who wrote: "My experiments with a glass model helped me along the way and I soon recognized that by employing glass, it is not an effect of light and shadow one wants to achieve, but a rich interplay of light reflections." Fully a third taller than its Friedrichstrasse predecessor, the building appears like a slim glass beacon in the drawings and in photographs of the model, in radical contrast to the low, earthbound buildings around, rendered as if made of clay.

The Concrete Office Building (1923), was also almost certainly designed for a specific Berlin site, now unknown. Not a new prototype, which the previous two projects represented, the office building design instead represented a new model for an existing building type. In place of the historicist styles of the characteristic Berlin block, Mies proposed a radically stripped-down architecture defined strictly by functional and structural concerns. The concrete building was to be supported by monolithic concrete

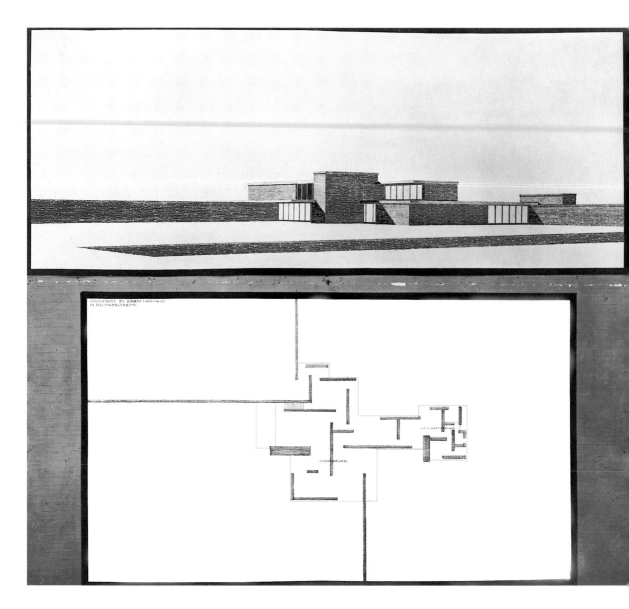

Brick Country House Project, 1924
Above: Perspective view (original lost)
Below: Plan (original lost)

columns and cantilevering beams carrying floor slabs. The beams gradually lengthen in the higher stories, thus enlarging the upper floor areas and avoiding the regularity of a mathematical parallelepiped. The rendering otherwise recalls François Hennebique's schematic diagram of the system, pioneered in the late 19th century. The construction technique was characteristically used in warehouse and factory design. The ranks of horizontal windows show that the walls do not carry the load of the roof, but support only themselves. Mies was evidently also inspired by the 1903 Larkin Building; just as Frank Lloyd Wright had done, the walls were designed to receive the ranks of filing cabinets required by modern business, tucked underneath high windows distributing light throughout the interior. The building reflects the efficiencies of modern industrial capital, and proposes architecture as the outgrowth of those forces. Like Schinkel's nearby Bauakademie before it, it was neither a factory nor a conventional bourgeois

building type. Instead, the Concrete Office Building offered a new rendition of both, diagnosing the nature and types of wage labor in the 20th century. Its architect sought poetry from the distilled facts of modern industrial life.

The remaining two of Mies's five early conceptual projects were both residential villas for suburban or country settings surrounding Berlin. The first, the Concrete Country House (1923), proposed the same stripped-down architectural language for a residence that the Concrete Office Building had proposed for business. But away from the limits of an urban site, the concrete house stretched out in several directions, drawing landscape into its precincts. The building's roofs floated over its walls, thanks to the possibilities of cantilever construction in concrete. By contrast, the thin brick walls of the Brick Country House (1924) remained firmly rooted in the ground, but ran beyond the limits of the interior spaces to describe internalized landscape zones continuous with the 'rooms' of the inside. The openness of the ground plan is a record of Mies's debt to Frank Lloyd Wright, however radically advanced by the former. According to Mies's own statements, he strived for "a sequence of spatial effects." "The wall loses its enclosing character and serves exclusively to structure the organism of the house." By subjugating walls to rhythmic dynamics rather than using them merely as boundaries of space, Mies created—in correspondence to De Stijl principles, a dynamic spatial composition.

1925–1927 ▸ Exhibition "The Dwelling"

Weissenhofsiedlung, Master Plan and Apartment Block, Am Weissenhof 14-20; Glass Room; The Materials Show
▸ Stuttgart, Germany

Mies apartment block, entry façade
Mercedes-Benz advertisement, c. 1928

In 1925 the *German Werkbund*, supported by the City of Stuttgart, began to plan a modern building exhibition to take place in Stuttgart. Mies was entrusted with the artistic leadership for the entire exhibition. His first task was the master plan of a new housing estate, designed as a series of low cubic buildings encircling and terracing the hill on which they were to be built. An early clay model for the scheme shows an organic composition of small buildings with shared terraces between. Despite many revisions, the constructed settlement presented to the public in 1927 as *Weissenhofsiedlung*, retained much of this original design. Because of its pure geometric shape, its flat roofs and its overall white appearance, opponents of the new style ridiculed it as "Arabville" and "Bolshevist Barracks." Mies also compiled the list of architects invited to participate in the project, among them international representatives of *Neues Bauen* like Walter Gropius, the brothers Taut, Le Corbusier, Mart Stam and J.J.P. Oud, Hans Scharoun, Ludwig Hilberseimer, Josef Frank, and, as guests of honor, forerunners of the modern age, Hans Poelzig and Peter Behrens.

Mies's apartment block was the most prominent building of the estate, sited on the highest part of the hill. The long, thin block was constructed using a steel construction frame that was independent of the interior dividing walls. The units could be divided up into varying sizes, and partitions could be added or removed. The fabric of the walls was concrete block. Among other items designed by Mies for one of his sample apartments, the famous cantilever chair was to become a classic of modern furniture design.

A separate component of the same *Werkbund* exhibition, the Materials Show, occupied exhibition space in the city center, displaying modern fittings and furnishings as well as household appliances. Of a number of individual exhibitions designed with collaborator Lilly Reich, Mies's Glass Room was perhaps the most striking. A residential installation including entry foyer, winter garden, living room, study, and library, the exhibit placed simple but conventional furnishings against the novelty of full-height colored glass partition walls. The stretched fabric ceiling was lit from above, producing a luminous field over the whole. An additional element was a small sealed glass chamber containing a sculpture by Wilhelm Lehmbruck. The combination of familiar and unfamiliar elements suggests Mies's and Reich's conception of the promise of modern architecture: a combination of new materials, new building techniques, and traditional needs.

In this exhibit created for the German glass industry, Mies and Reich tested the different effects of colored glass walls. The designers used several tints of reflective plate glass, including milky white, gray, bottle green, and clear glass, creating an overall effect that was both dynamic and unexpected. Throughout the exhibit, which was designed as a series of 'rooms,' all visible from one another through the glass partitions, the Lehmbruck torso and winter garden gesture to art and nature as contemplative subjects, a longstanding theme of German aesthetics. In addition, various household

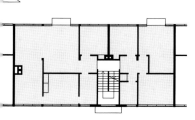

Floor plan of typical apartment units

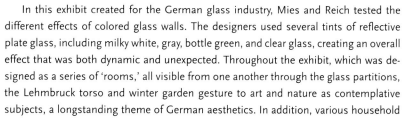

Garden façade of apartment block, c. 1927

Left:
View of apartment interior, c. 1927

Below:
MR chair

items filled the individual 'rooms'. The project counter-posed the unexpected effects of tinted glass walls against the entirely 'normal' appearance of household objects. This strategy of juxtaposing the conventional and the unexpected can be linked to Mies's earlier connections to Berlin Dada, with its startling assemblages of familiar objects in unfamiliar combinations. The Glass Room is currently regarded as a milestone in Mies's development, thanks to its membraneous walls, fluid transitions, and open ground plan. It constitutes the first clear indication of the spatial concept that would be developed further by Mies in the Barcelona Pavilion and the Villa Tugendhat.

Although the *Werkbund* exhibition lasted only three months, it drew the attention of approximately half a million visitors from all over the world, and paved the way for Mies's entry into the international scene, both as administrator and as pioneer and theoretician of avant-garde architecture. The exhibition also fuelled the protests of the right wing, protests that would grow increasingly more militant in the years that followed.

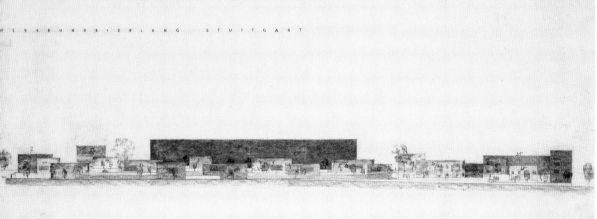

above:
[vi]ew of estate, with Mies block as 'city crown,' 1927

[b]elow:
[e]arly pencil sketch of estate in elevation, 1926

1927–1930 · Lange and Esters Houses
Wilhelmshofallee 91 and 97, Krefeld, Germany

nterior of Lange House

Not long after the completion of Mies's first modern brick house on the banks of the Neisse River in Guben for Erich Wolf in 1927, silk manufacturers Hermann Lange and Josef Esters commissioned Mies to build their houses on adjoining lots in the western city of Krefeld. The two clients were lifelong friends and business partners; Hermann Lange was also a well known art-collector with close connections to the Berlin avant-garde.

Continuing investigations begun at the Wolf House, Mies used these commissions to further develop a residential design technique that coordinated rhythmic movement through space with strategic views out to the landscape and into surrounding rooms. Large windows and doors provide close connection to the outside and several terraces at the garden side of the house. Without the drama of a panoramic view to conclude the sequence, as at Wolf and at the Riehl House (and later at the Tugendhat House), the Krefeld houses are more internally focused than their predecessors. Planned as fraternal 'twins,' both houses have a similar spatial order. In contrast to Mies's Glass Room project in Stuttgart, these houses cling to the bourgeois domestic typology of distinctly bounded rooms. And yet, a shared spatial choreography can be identified with projects both earlier and later, one that Mies would continue to pursue for many years in a variety of applications, and with rich results.

The Esters and Lange buildings were both surfaced in dark brick; but they are only partially bearing-wall structures. They were among the first modern buildings to free brick from its load-bearing function; their facades were therefore extremely unusual for the time. Much of the load-bearing structure within was steel, tailored to an extremely complicated design. This permanent metal scaffolding allowed the architect to cut large openings in the exterior walls-openings far too large for bearing wall construction to sustain. Much to the chagrin of his structural engineer, Ernst Walther, Mies let the

Lange House from garden, with Esters House
beyond

Right:
Lange House
Ground floor plan

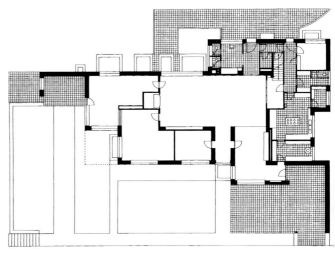

Left:

Lange House
Living hall with built-in vitrine

Esters House
Ground floor plan

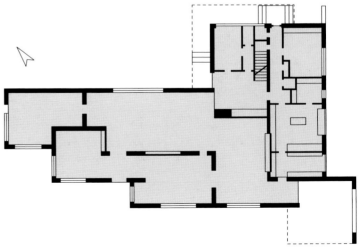

Mies sketching the Esters House, around 1927–1928 in his office at Am Karlsbad 24 in Berlin-Tiergarten

spatial design dictate the structural calculations, following formal and experiential dictates rather than traditional constructional logic. This is expressed in the large openings that seemingly liberate the wall from its load-bearing function, in the process contradicting the implied character of the façade and its engineering. The structural contortions of the Krefeld villas may have been part of Mies's exploration of De Stijl planning principles, where the necessity for overlap and offset between parts—the conscious communication of a structure's evasion of rational logics, must be made explicit. Hermann Lange's initial conversations with Theo van Doesburg and Cornelis van Eesteren on the subject of a house commission for Krefeld indicates a convergence of interests in this direction.

The clients were directors of the United Silk Weaveries (Vereinigte Seidenwebereien A.G.), a company that continued over a period of years to provide Mies and Lilly Reich with significant commissions. Mies built factory buildings for their Krefeld plant, collaborated with Reich on a number of exhibition installations for the silk industry, remodeled the apartment interior of Lange's daughter Mildred in Berlin, and even designed a house for the son of Hermann, Ulrich Lange, for an outlying suburb of Krefeld. This project was never built. Both brick villas belong today to the city of Krefeld, open to the public as part of Krefeld's art museums and used for contemporary art exhibitions.

1928–1929 ᐧ Barcelona Pavilion
International Exhibition
Avinguda del Marquès de Comillas, Barcelona, Spain

Following his successful administration of the 1927 *Werkbund* exhibition in Stuttgart, Mies was entrusted by the government of the German *Reich* with the artistic management and erection of buildings for all the German sections at the 1929 Universal Exhibition in Barcelona. He was offered the commission in 1928, under uncertain economic conditions and severe time constraints. His design for an independent exhibition pavilion, and his collaboration with Lilly Reich and others for a series of industrial exhibition installations were all executed in less than a year.

The Pavilion of German Representation, known as 'The Barcelona Pavilion', is one of Mies's principal works. In the wake of WWI and of the economic recovery that followed the 1924 Dawes Plan, the building was to represent the new Germany: democratic, culturally progressive, prospering, and thoroughly pacifist. With this building the German government was to offer the world a lyrical self-portrait through the medium of modern architecture. Constructed for ceremonial and representational purposes, the building was used for the official opening of the German section of the exhibition, when the Spanish king and queen visited the building in state.

Mies's decisive steps, for the first time carried out entirely at the Barcelona Pavilion, consisted of the realization of the "free plan" and the "floating room." Like an antique temple, the building rested on a plinth of travertine, with a southern U-shaped enclosure of the same material leading to a small service annex. A large water basin stretched towards the south-east, its floor-slabs projecting over the edge and giving the impression that the water's surface continues under the plinth, connecting outside and inside. A second, smaller basin was situated on the north side, where the plinth was bordered by another U-shaped wall made of green marble. The building's roof plate was carried by cruciformed, chrome-clad columns, giving the impression of a hovering roof and disclosing the non supporting character of the walls. Plates of high-grade stone-materials like Tinos-Marble, Vert-Antique Marble and onyx doré as well as tinted glass (grey, green, white and translucent) performed the exclusive function of precious spatial dividers, sliding under the roof plate and creating a floating transition between inside and outside. It can be seen that Mies combined two of his Stuttgart innovations here: the metal-framed structure of his *Weissenhof* apartment building and the translucent walls of his Glass Room.

The circulation routes through the varied spaces of the building complex include Mies's now-familiar combination of rhythmic movement coordinated with carefully-composed views. Ascending the stairs to the building's podium across a wide plaza, the visitor stands before the larger outdoor pool planted with water lilies, then turns 180 degrees to enter the building's 'interior'—at this point defined by the roof plate. A narrow entry corridor flanked by green marble slabs on the left and the eastern outer glass wall on the right leads into the main interior space: a rectangular space cut by one long plane of onyx doré in front of which chairs and table sit on a black carpet, shielded from the glass window-wall behind by a rich red silk curtain. Left of the onyx wall, is a 'light-wall': a translucent light box of milky glass lit artificially from within. Like

Pavilion seen from plaza, 1929

News photograph of King Alfonso XIII of
Spain conversing with Commissioner Georg
von Schnitzler beside the small pool, May,
1929

ll other wall planes, this box of light rises from floor to ceiling, recalling the "Light-
architecture" of Weimar Berlin's commercial centers, with their brilliantly-lit shop vitri-
nes. Other wall elements break up the regularity of the space, and the outer, right-hand
wall, changing from glass to marble, leads the visitor further into a small court open to
the sky with the smaller pool already mentioned. In this pool, raised on a base, stands
the over-life-size figure "Der Morgen" (The Morning) by sculptor Georg Kolbe: the
bronze sculpture of a woman rising from the water and gesturing to the rising sun. In
its austere dark green setting, the statue resembles a figure in a photomontage, the
built version of one of Willi Baumeister's evocative figure compositions. Turning left
past the statue, the visitor reenters the building behind the beautiful slab of onyx, with
view down to the light box in the depth of the building; one can also leave the interior
here, walking down the long side of the back of the building and away from the statue.
Here, an exit to the right led originally to the "Spanish Town," an assemblage of
vernacular architectural styles on the hill above. Alternatively, the visitor can turn left
into a covered open space ouside the milk-glass light box and overlooking the large
open pool again. A travertine bench on the long side of this pool invites a rest and a
look back across the long plaza to the exhibition proper. A brief glance to the left, and

Interior, looking along onyx wall toward light wall
Contemporary photograph (after 1986)

the visitor is greeted by the Kolbe statue at the end of the western corridor. Critics at the time characterized the entire assemblage as an oasis, inviting the visitor for a mo mentary pause' from the frenzied activity of a busy international exposition.

Planned as an exhibition pavilion, the building was intended to exist only for a limi ted time. Significant difficulties during the building's construction were attributed to an incredibly narrow time-frame, budget cuts and last but not least, relatively outdated building methods on site which led to diverse structural flaws, most notably the poorly built roof and resulting water damage. Completed in May 1929, the building was torn down in early 1930.

Thanks also to the information relayed by the photographs, the building was recon structed, after careful study, by a talented group of Spanish architects between 1983 and 1986. The power of the original image has seemed to challenge even contem porary photographers, as the building has been repeatedly photographed since its completion.

Interior showing onyx wall and glazed wall to courtyard.
Contemporary photograph (after 1986)

Left:
Floor plan

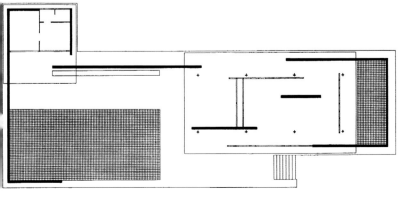

1928–1930·Tugendhat House

Schwarzfeldgasse 45, Brünn, Czechoslovakia (today Ul. Cernopolní 45, Brno, Czech Republic)

Sketch showing the garden façade with the willow tree outside dining niche, other plantings, and automobiles on Cernopolní Street

In 1928, as preparations for the Barcelona exhibition began, another important commission came into Mies's office. A wealthy industrialist couple, Fritz and Grete Tugendhat, wanted a family villa on a plot of land received as a wedding gift from the bride's parents, in the Moravian provincial capital of Brno. Brno was a center for modern architecture in Czechoslovakia at the time. The choice of Mies may have been due to the Tugendhat's bonds, as German-Bohemian Jews, to German culture, living in a town with a large German population. Grete Tugendhat had lived for some years in Berlin, where she was a regular visitor at Perls House, realized by Mies in 1911–1912. Since then she had kept a close eye on the artistic development of the architect.

Mies designed the building through 1928 and 1929, and construction began in 1929. Money was not an issue for the Tugendhats and they were prepared to give Mies a free hand even with the interior design of the house. For Mies, therefore, the commission offered a unique opportunity to realize in close detail his own ideas about architecture and furniture design without any restrictions from his client. Extending some of the ideas of the Barcelona Pavilion, Mies nevertheless designed the house around the dramatically different needs of a family. Instead of a circuitous ceremonial route through the building's spaces, the Tugendhat House provided a combination of both freer and more restricted spaces to accommodate domestic use.

The villa is situated on a steeply falling hillside, making a very modest impression from the street side. The entry approach leads directly to a framed aperture that offers a spectacular panorama over the old city of Brno. This view is flanked by the garage on the right, and a building mass laid out parallel to the street on the left. Entering the house via its main entrance, concealed behind a curving milk-glass wall, the visitor finds himself on the top floor, where a square foyer offers access to a private area with conventionally enclosed bedrooms and a roof terrace. A flight of stairs, following the

Left page:
Looking toward terrace door, with dining room to the right
Contemporary photograph (after 1985)

Entry facade from southeast on Cernopolní Street

Upper roof terrace with hemicycle bench and pergola beyond
Contemporary photograph (after 1985)

urve of the milk-glass wall, descends to the main floor where the open living area
xtends over a surface of 280 square meters. This space freely merges entrance hall,
ving room, dining area, work area with library, and lounge corner into a single space.
n addition, a projection booth for showing films, and a long winter garden flank this
oom on north and east sides respectively. The living area is clearly separated by fixed
oom dividers from more restricted spaces for domestic use, such as the kitchen,
antry, and servants quarters.

Mies used the same design principle of the free plan and fluid space that he used
t Barcelona. Conceptually, however, the dualistic play of columns and planes was
eplaced by an investigation of space as simultaneously integrated and subdivided.
Here, a greater array of elements joined the cruciform columns: a single slab of onyx,
unning from floor to ceiling, parallel to the length of the house and dividing the front
ving area from the working space, and a half-cylinder covered with Makassar-Ebony,
vhich screened the dining area from the rest of the space. Other elements structuring
ne main living area were a series of silk curtains in muted shades and the furniture, all
f it designed by Mies in cooperation with Lilly Reich. For the villa in particular he
lesigned the "Brno-chair," the "Tugendhat-arm-chair" and the glass table. And like in
he Barcelona Pavilion there was also a sculpture at Villa Tugendhat: a female torso by
Mies van der Rohe's friend, Wilhelm Lehmbruck. This was another version of the same
iece that graced Mies's 1927 Glass Room interior.

In Brno, Mies also followed the idea of visual connection between interior and
xterior. The living area opens out on the sloping side, with gigantic floor to ceiling

**Main entry door and stairway leading down to
main living floor.**

View of house from bottom of garden
Contemporary photograph (after 1985)

Macassar dining niche, with door to terrace at the far left edge

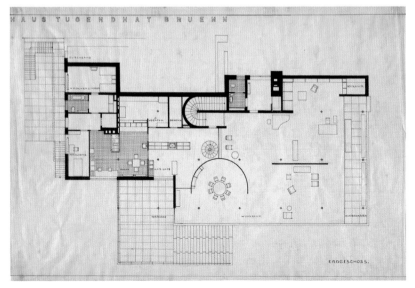

Left:
Lower level plan

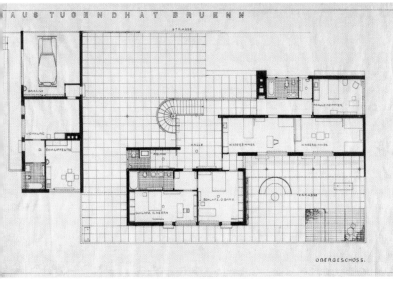

Library niche with 'curtain wall' to the left

Left:
Upper level (entry level) floor plan, with bedrooms and service areas
Staff quarters lie behind garage; family bedrooms occupy an independent wing with access to upper terrace.

Winter garden

panoramic windows creating an interior room that was also a terrace, suspended, as if in the branches of an enormous weeping willow that stood just outside the dining area. This effect was enhanced by two sinking windows that, powered by electricity, could be retracted fully into the floor. By this means Mies combined interior and landscape, an impression that is sustained throughout this remarkably generous yet intimate space. Access to the garden was through a second single door past the length of the dining niche, where stairs led down into the garden. Mies's constructed addition to the Henke House in Essen, which was completed in the very same year, took the aspect of transition between inside and out to the next step: its glass garden front included a single glass sheet nine meters long that retracted in one single plane into the floor of the addition, allowing the Henke's free access to the sculpture garden just outside, and turning their dining room into a terrace.

If the Barcelona Pavilion found nearly unanimous approval in the press, the Tugendhat House generated considerable uncertainty about the premises on which modern architecture was based. "It is like the Parthenon. Photos don't say anything about this building!" rejoiced Philip Johnson after a visit at Brno. Anything but enthusiastic, however, was the judgement of Marxist advocates of modern architecture. They saw the Tugendhat House as betraying basic principles of radical modernism, with their emphasis on economies of budget and scale. Indeed, the villa Tugendhat was hardly to be seen as contributing to the solution of social problems. The building's size, materials, appointments, and most of all budget unambiguously declared its status as a work of art and private palace. The building is reported to have cost ten

times the budget of Le Corbusier's contemporaneous (and already expensive) Villa Savoye; the cost of the onyx wall alone equivalent to that of a family home. The Czech avant-garde author and photographer Karel Teige therefore declared the building an example of the wrong direction in modern architecture and called it "the peak of modern snobbism."

The Tugendhat House was occupied by the family for little more than seven years. The family emigrated in 1938, in the run-up to the Nazi-German invasion. As "unappropriated Jewish property" the house was confiscated by the National Socialists and registered in 1942 in the estate register as property of the Reich; during the war it housed occasionally a design office of the aircraft engine company "Ostmark," but by then the ebony wall and the Lehmbruck sculpture had already vanished. In 1945 the Red Army took quarters in the villa. In 1950 the house became property of the Czechoslovakian state and used as an institute for physiotherapy. In 1963 the Villa was declared cultural monument, restored in 1985, and in 2001 listed in the UNESCO International Cultural and Natural Heritage List.

1929·Alexanderplatz competition
Not realized ▸ Berlin-Mitte, Germany

Photomontage of Alexanderplatz competition design, 1929

In early 1929 Mies was invited to take part in a competition for re-designing of the Alexanderplatz, in which "the passage of traffic" was "the primary and major element, and the formal design and functional form is only of secondary significance." Ignoring these competition guidelines, Mies proposed an open public space and a larger assemblage of urban office and retail buildings removed from the street edge. Asymmetrically grouped around the square, these rectangular prisms, sheathed in reflective and translucent glass, were to be seen as objects of both art and consumer culture. The message was clear: At this important urban juncture, in a busy commercial and entertainment node, space was not to be shaped solely by traffic patterns but to follow the formal logic entailed in crafting public space according to modernist principles.

    Although the competition drawings are schematic at best, the execution of these buildings would no doubt have followed the lead set by Mies's Stuttgart Bank and Office Building Project of 1928 (unbuilt), in which the ground floor was to be sheathed in clear glass, the floors above in milky or translucent glass. A close parallel can also be found in Mies's project for the Saul Adam Department Store intended for a site on the corner of Friedrichstrasse and Leipzigerstrasse in Berlin of 1929 (also unbuilt). In all these glass building projects, the skin was intended to function as a light box, both for interior and exterior use. The milky glass surface would have provided generous, even light to the interior; it would also have provided a backlight for advertising signage affixed to the building's skin, as shown in one of the model photographs of the Stuttgart building.

1933 · Reichsbank Extension

Not realized ▸ Kurstr. 36-40, Berlin-Mitte, Germany

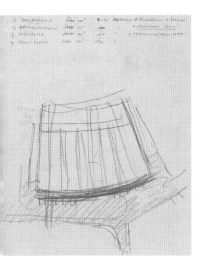

View from Spree canal, showing end of wings (the connecting bar between them does not appear in this view).

Early sketch of Reichsbank

Again invited to compete for a major building commission in Berlin, Mies entered the Reichsbank Extension competition in early 1933, along with twenty-nine others, among them Walter Gropius. Located across the street from the existing Reichsbank, the building represented a massive enlargement of the existing institution, increasing the presence of the central bank and bridging the distance between the old building and the Spree Canal.

Mies's building was connected by subterranean passage to the older building. This allowed his proposal to stand alone on its site as a single independent block, vaguely reminiscent of his Concrete Office Building of 1923 in its massing, its horizontal articulation, and its symmetry. The building plan consists of three bars laid out perpendicular to the entry façade. The smooth sweep of this main street facade binds the three bars together through a large central entry hall or foyer. The bars protrude like individual building masses over the Spree canal on the opposite side; a second connecting bar was inset, facilitating internal circulation and creating interior light courts. The building contained a monumental ceremonial entry, up one of two pendant staircases just inside the entry and into the massive glass-walled lobby above. From this lobby three large banking halls filled the three wings perpendicular to the streetfront. On the floors above, all of these areas housed offices; on the roof was a generous roof terrace and dining rooms for the office workers and officials.

Although Mies received an award for his design, the National Socialist government rejected the competition results. Hitler himself favored a bulky monumental building, designed by Heinrich Wolff, director of the building department of the Reichsbank.

1939–1958 › Illinois Institute of Technology
Chicago, Illinois, USA

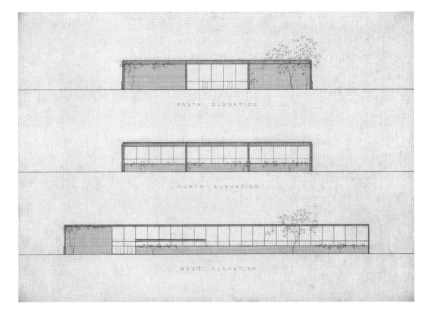

The master plan of a campus for the Illinois Institute of Technology presented Mies with a challenging commission immediately upon his arrival in a new country, with an entirely new kind of infrastructure and a new sort of architectural and engineering culture. Mies quickly arrived at a solution to the problem posed. Rather than attempting to continue earlier investigations from his Berlin context, he rapidly shifted gear over the first two years of his IIT tenure. After designing a master plan for the campus, Mies began work on individual buildings, many of which were built over the next twenty years.

Only one group of projects from the German years would seem to have direct bearing on his Chicago campus: the designs executed for the silk industry in Krefeld in the 1930s. Although the first of these was a factory building, the second was an office and administration building that resembled a factory, recalling the much earlier Concrete Office Building that had equated white collar work with factory labor. It thus comes as no surprise to find the IIT campus buildings often articulated in the same way: as factory buildings easily adapted for the different activities of learning and professional training. Mies's own deployment of the term *Baukunst* (the art of building) from the early 1920s illustrates his refusal of traditional high-low distinctions in architectural culture, although he was not consistent in this refusal. Crown Hall, the architecture building, notably evaded this logic; the architectural studio rather embedded the factory workshop in a building replete with ceremonial intent.

True to the systematic implications of factory architecture, Mies devised a modular system for the ordering of the campus. The system depended on a structural model of

Ensemble of Navy Building (Alumni memorial Hall) in the far distance, Metallurgy and Chemical Engineering Building (Perlstein Hall) in the center, and the Chemistry Building (Wishnick Hall) on the right.

Right:
IIT Chapel

24 feet in both directions, laid out over the breadth of the site. Individual buildings then followed this dimensional constraint. In addition, Mies embraced a new design system and a new kind of architectural expression for these buildings. Abandoning the dual system of structure versus enclosure, so prevalent in his work in Germany, Mies embraced the steel construction frame as a unitary system within which spatial dividers conformed to a prevailing geometric and modular order. Developing this language as far as he could in the course of building the IIT campus, Mies developed consistent details for joining the brick fabric of the walls with the steel structure that held them in place and supported the roof.

The Library and Administration Building (1944–1945) would have represented a substantial addition to the corpus of buildings, but sadly remained unbuilt. Combining offices, assembly space, library stacks, reading room, garden courtyard, and single- and double-height zones, the building displays the flexibility of Mies's new system, along with a quasi-Japanese ascetic grace.

Concert Hall Collage, 1942

Mies did not embark, in his American years, on a single intense period of theoretical
work, as he had perhaps done with the 'five projects' of the early 1920s in Berlin. Nevertheless, his theoretical work continued in a number of unbuilt projects that grounded
his new design ideas in their Chicago context. The later version of the Resor House
design might be included in this group, although it originated in a real commission.
Many of these conceptual projects were partly executed with students at IIT over a
period of years.

The project for a Museum for a Small City (1940–1943), grew from an IIT student
thesis and a competition sponsored by *Architectural Forum* in 1943. In this case, Mies
continued to deploy the design system used so frequently in his German years: the
separation of structure from enclosure, and the corresponding use of a column grid
and freely-composed spatial dividers. This project might be said to represent the last
of Mies's German works. Hints of a future direction can nevertheless be clearly traced
particularly in the way in which the auditorium occupies an uncomfortable position
within the matrix of columns. Removing the column grid from its interior, Mies added
a pair of trusses to the roof of the auditorium, to free the space of internal support.
Thus began an investigation into large-scale superstructure that would occupy much
of his attention in Chicago, leading to the development of clear span structures.

The second of these conceptual projects, the Concert Hall design (1941–1942)
records Mies's encounter with the American industrial architecture of the mid-West
and his increasing interest in architectural superstructures separate from the spatial
enclosures they created. The project consists of a single photocollage known in two

Museum for a Small City Project
Sketch showing suspended roof panel over
auditorium, 1942

Right:
Museum for a Small City Project
Plan, 1943

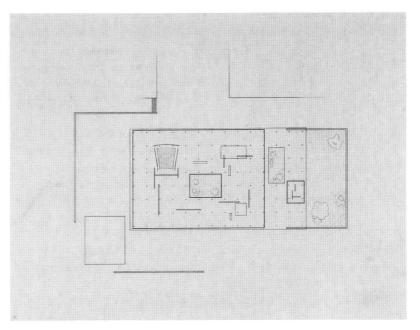

versions, and can be considered a reflection by the architect on his new environment, rather than a proposal intended for construction. Using a photograph of Albert Kahn's vast Glenn L. Martin airplane factory, Mies superimposed cut paper to suggest a gathering space or auditorium whose abstract surfaces were suspended from or housed by the surrounding metallic armature. The project can be taken as prophetic of several designs that followed; the later Theatre Design (1947) depicts a related scheme.

A related interest in interiors free of all structural support appeared some years later in The 50 x 50 House (1951–1952), a theoretical project. In this case, the roof was to be suspended, not from above, but from single columns placed at the midpoint of each side of a square. This deceptively simple design required complex engineering, since it introduced a double cantilever at each roof corner, maximizing roof loads at the points of least support. Nevertheless, this scheme represented the beginnings of a new idea about clear span structures that Mies would continue to pursue until the very end of his long life, culminating in the New National Gallery in Berlin.

Right page above:
Chicago Convention Hall Project
Photocollage with multiple photographic reproductions of 1952 Republican National Convention, and fabric replica of U.S. flag. 1953

Right page below:
Chicago Convention Hall Project
Model with patterned curtain wall, 1953–1954

Model of 50 x 50 House, 1952

The largest conceptual project attempted by Mies with students from IIT was that for a Convention Hall (1953–1954) in Chicago. Here Mies proposed his own version of the thick roof of the Martin factory used in his Concert Hall collage. Here it was transposed into a space frame megastructure; a vast open space with no internal divisions, to house large conventions similar to the many national and international exhibitions to which Mies had contributed over the course of his professional life. The most famous rendering of this project is a photocollage of the project's substantial model, which includes photographs of the crowd at Chicago's Republican National Convention of 1952, mounted like wallpaper over the breadth of the collage, which was also equipped with a American flag made of printed fabric.

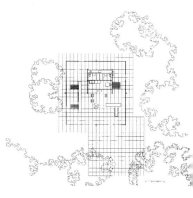

Plan of 50 x 50 House, 1952

1945–1951 ▸ Farnsworth House

River Road, Plano, Illinois, USA

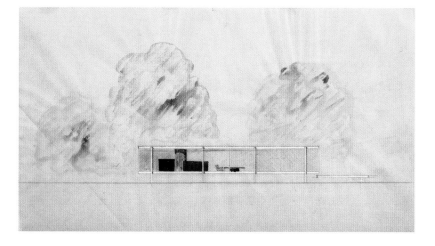

Early study with watercolor by Mies and
Edward Duckett, 1945

This entirely open glass pavilion is Mies's most radical domestic design. Meant to
serve as a weekend getaway house on a secluded wooded site near the Fox River, the
house deploys eight I-shaped steel columns to support roof and floor frameworks.
Engineered for maximum lightness, the mullions that stretch from roof to floor between window planes also help support the floor plate. The steel is highly finished and
painted white, in dramatic contrast to the black enamel clothing IIT's steel frames.

In an interview given a few years later, Mies explained the principles of the glass
pavilion as they had been realized in the Farnsworth house: "Nature, too, shall live its
own life. We must beware not to disrupt it with the color of our houses and interior
fittings. Yet we should attempt to bring nature, houses, and human beings together
into a higher unity. If you view nature through the glass walls of the Farnsworth House,
it gains a more profound significance than if viewed from outside. That way more is
said about nature—it becomes a part of a larger whole." Mies concluded his work in
domestic design with this building and the contemporaneous unbuilt scheme for a
"50 x 50" house; he seems to have had little else to say about domestic construction
after the conclusion of these two open pavilions, both designed for living in direct
contemplation of nature.

Designed and built for a single woman, the successful Chicago doctor Edith Farnsworth, the house was created over several years in intensive consultation with its client.
Farnsworth began with great enthusiasm, not only for the project but also for the architect's personality. The client was bitterly disappointed after the building's completion,
when its abstract simplicity proved surprisingly difficult to live with. These and other
facts led to a break between architect and client. Disputes about the value of the finished building included complaints about the poor ventilation of the interior, and cost
overruns. Nevertheless, the Farnsworth House stands out as one of Mies's most re-
markable buildings for its combined simplicity, conceptual elegance, and beauty.

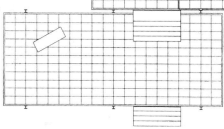

Side view of house in autumn
Contemporary photograph

Left:
Plan

House from the direction of the Fox River
Contemporary photograph

Left:
View of entry from terrace

1948–1951▸Lake Shore Drive Apartments

860–880 Lakeshore Drive, Chicago, Illinois, USA

Left page:
General view toward lake

Right:
View to lake between canopy that connects buildings.

Below:
Detail of structure and cladding at corner

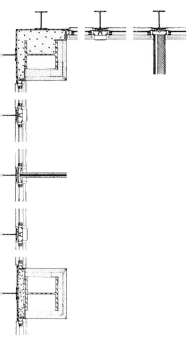

Of the many high-rise buildings that dominated Mies's American years, the first apartment buildings constructed on the banks of Lake Michigan rank among his most important. Mies executed this project with Herbert Greenwald. Just as continued experiment at IIT had led to the development of a set of resolved technical solutions for steel detailing, so did the first set of Lake Shore Drive apartments show how Mies had begun to resolve the challenges of steel-frame high-rise construction. Obligated to cover the steel structure with two inches of fireproofing concrete, Mies then sheathed the concrete in more metal, giving the outer face of the building a skin that reflected and expressed the structure underneath. In addition, the metal exterior responded to important functional requirements, stiffening the skin and preventing warping from heat and wind loads. Developed initially for these 26-story buildings, a similar solution was found for the much taller office building type that came to dominate Mies's practice in the 1960s.

View of lobby

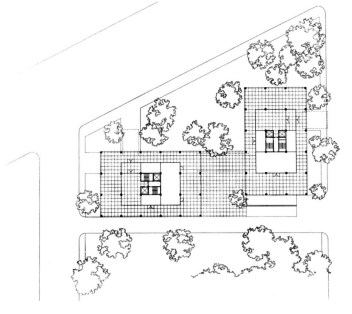

Ground level plans

1950–1956▸Crown Hall

IIT Campus ▸ **South Federal Street, Chicago, Illinois, USA**

Frontal view at dusk

Certainly the most extraordinary building constructed by Mies at IIT, Crown Hall differs notably from other campus buildings. Having dictated a language and ordering system for the entire campus, Mies then arrogated to himself the right to break out of the system in his design for the architecture building. Instead of an integrated system of structure and enclosure within the constraints of steel framing, Crown Hall represents a final iteration of his many investigations of a one-way structural system that left the building interior entirely column-free. This was possible by suspending the roof from the underside of four large steel plate girders, which in turn are carried by eight exterior steel columns. This creates a hall 18 feet high enclosing an area 120 x 220 feet with a façade of glass panes that span from floor to ceiling. Outside the entrance, the lower parts of the glass walls are sandblasted. The structural system of Crown Hall resembles that used in the Farnsworth House, but rendered at a monumental scale. The building is raised by 6 feet on a platform with a grand flight of stairs at the entrance; a

typical feature of Mies's later work. The raised platform allows openings at ground level to provide natural light and ventilation for the workshops and seminar rooms in the basement. The architectural studios occupy the main floor of the building, ranks of tables stretching out in a vast open space. An ongoing preoccupation of Miesian modernism—complete spatial freedom with full enclosure—has been realized. More than any engineering victory, though, Crown Hall aims for the idea of liberation from mythological bonds, as understood after Nietzsche and advocated by the avant-garde since the turn of the century; a kind of mythical liberation no longer fully comprehensible in a post Holocaust world.

Mies van der Rohe called Crown Hall his most perfect work. It was for him "the clearest statement of his philosophy of a universal space building." After the construction of Crown Hall, Mies turned his attention to the development of a two-way structure that would combine the column-free interior with a bilaterally symmetrical structure.

1954–1958 · Seagram Building

52nd Street / 375 Park Avenue, New York City,
New York, USA

eft page:
Overall view looking downtown (south).

ew across plaza fountains, with Skidmore,
wings & Merrill's Lever House beyond

The commission for the Seagram Building on Park Avenue, New York, came into Mies's office thanks to the efforts of Phyllis Lambert, daughter of Seagram owner Samuel Bronfman. According to the design guidelines, the building needed to be not only suitable for its high profile site, but also extremely sophisticated. It was Lambert's task to find a suitable architect, and she looked at an illustrious group that included Frank Lloyd Wright, Walter Gropius and Le Corbusier. Philip Johnson's advocacy of Mies in his 1947 exhibition at the Museum of Modern Art had played an important role in bringing Mies to public attention. After Mies had secured the commission, he brought Johnson (now trained as an architect) into the project as an associate.

Left page:
Corner view of curtain wall; Lever House on right.

Right:
View of side entry on 52nd St

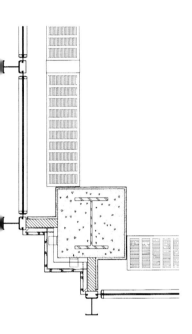

Detail of structure and cladding at corner

The Seagram building was Mies's first foray into tall office building construction, after an apprenticeship in high-rise apartment buildings like the Lake Shore Drive and Promontory Apartments in Chicago. It was considerably bigger than these earlier projects, and involved a central urban site in America's most prominent city. Mies responded with an extraordinary urban gesture, only possible to appreciate in relation to its mid-1950s context of rampant economic expansion. He removed the vertical slab of the building from the street edge and inserted a generous open plaza at the front of the site, thus neglecting strictly economic considerations and dedicating the most valuable part of the site to public use. The resulting, rather luxurious distance between building and street set off the building to maximum advantage. Mies thus distanced himself from both New York urban morphology, lot line development, and the conventional economics of skyscraper construction. This decision recalls his Alexanderplatz competition of 1929, in which he similarly ignored the prevailing urbanism of traffic engineering and lot line architecture, placing buildings that installed their own order

over the city, as much as they accepted the dictates of context. Similarly, the Seagram Building rises against the civic gesture of its open plaza, with generous outdoor seating and two large fountains. Thus Mies created an alternative urbanism, one in which big building also paid its debt to the city by fostering civic life. The Seagram plaza had two direct effects: it influenced the revision of New York's zoning codes in 1961; this in turn led to a higher tax premium for the building's low floor area ratio.

The broad plane of the Seagram plaza sweeps through the entry doors into the building's lobby, eschewing strict boundaries between inside and out. In addition, the white ceiling of the lobby stretches out through and over the entry doors, further eroding the edge between inside and out and maintaining continuity between the horizontal sweep of the plaza and the glazed space of the lobby. In the office spaces above most of them furnished by Johnson, flexible floor plans were lit throughout with luminous ceiling panels, harking back to Mies's Stuttgart Glass Room from 1927 with its luminous fabric ceilings (a fact that their designer, Philip Johnson, may well have remembered from personal experience). In addition to window panes of gray topaz glass for sun and heat protection, the window coverings were regulated so that the

building's Venetian blinds could be fixed in a limited number of positions for the sake of visual consistency from the outside. And finally, the detailing of the exterior surface was carefully determined by the desired exterior expression. Here, as at the Lake Shore Drive Apartments, Mies sheathed the exterior in a non-structural metal skin, this time of bronze, that nevertheless articulated an idea about the building's structure that echoed but inflected the structural frame underneath. Again, additional vertical elements welded to the window panels increased the vertical articulation of the building at the same time that they stiffened the skin for installation and wind loading. Incorporated into the 39-floor construction are two side wings at the back, one ten floors high, the other four.

The Seagram Building, set back from the city grid, has nevertheless come to be seen as the quintessential 20th-century skyscraper. It provided a model for countless buildings erected in its wake, both on Park Avenue and, perhaps most notably, in the ranks of corporate high rises that line Sixth Avenue across town. In addition, Seagram provided a prototype for the sort of office building that Mies would build intensively over the next ten years.

1955–1963 · Lafayette Park
Detroit, Michigan, USA
▸ Ludwig Hilberseimer collaborator

A residential development with low- and high-rise buildings, Lafayette Park is a garden city project for downtown Detroit. It was designed by Mies with his long-time collaborator and IIT colleague Ludwig Hilberseimer, Mies's comrade-in-arms from years back in Berlin. Its assemblage of different building types recalls the IIT campus, reinterpreted as a residential development featuring apartment blocks, townhouses, and single-story rowhouses. Like the Lake Shore Drive Apartment Buildings, Mies executed this project with Herbert Greenwald and his development company, Metropolitan Structures. Greenwald's collaboration with Mies on a number of high-rise buildings marks a high point of architect-developer relations in the United States, and Lafayette Park was one of its successful results. Working with themes that had occupied Mies before, the complex included courtyard apartments, low-rise buildings, and high-rise apartments, all executed in a similar language of brick, steel, and glass.

Similarities between units distributed throughout the different building types attest Mies's effort to find prototypical solutions for the basic problems of modern living. For him, the problem of mass housing was, however, not solely one of economy or social rights; it was still an aesthetic and 'spiritual' problem that attempted to make architecture a foil for life in harmony with the environment, whether urban, semi-urban, or rural.

In 1959, Greenwald was killed in a plane crash, interrupting the progress of projects with which Mies's office was then involved. Lafayette Park was therefore not finished by Mies and Hilberseimer, and its further development was taken over by other architects. The last high-rise apartment buildings to Mies's design were completed in 1963.

View of low-rise housing with mature landscaping

Right Page:
General view showing low- and high-rise housing

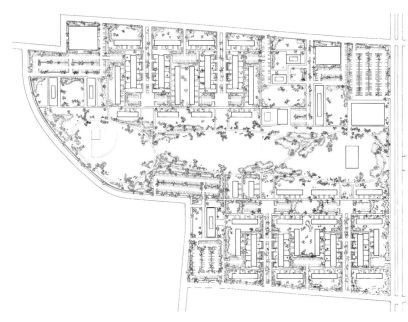

Site plan

1962–1968 › New National Gallery
Potsdamer Strasse 50, Berlin, Germany

Interior of pavilion

Left page:
Podium and roof with Matthias Church beyond

Called back to Berlin at the end of his career, Mies accepted the commission for the New National Gallery, an art museum to house contemporary work in Berlin's new Kulturforum, not far from the site of then-decimated Potsdamer Platz and the Berlin Wall. Also a stone's throw from Mies's now-destroyed office, the project must have had great attraction for the aging architect. It summarizes themes that had occupied Mies over many years of practice, returning him both literally and metaphorically to the land of Karl Friedrich Schinkel, his old homeland—and to his own beginnings.

Pursuing an idea that had occupied him at least since the 50 x 50 House of 1951, Mies developed the design as a square pavilion with glass sides and no interior supports. Instead, eight columns on the exterior would hold the massive roof over the floor and off the glass walls. Working with designs already developed for the Bacardí Office Building for Santiago, Cuba (unbuilt) and the private Georg Schäfer Museum for Schweinfurt (also unbuilt), Mies realized the design in Berlin in its grandest iteration. In response to the strain of the double cantilever at the corners of the roof plate, a result of the column-free corners, Mies and his engineers devised an ingenious solution. The massive roof was constructed of enormous steel box beams of different grades of steel with varying strengths, welded into a single coffered plate. Thus the steel at the corners of the building could remain the same thickness as steel that was subject to lower stresses in other parts of the roof plate. The roof was assembled on the ground and jacked into place with the aid of eight hydraulic jacks over the course of a single day. Mies sat underneath in a white Mercedes.

Entry façade on Potsdamer Straße

Right:
View of sculpture garden, lower level, with pavilion roof to left

The genesis of the original idea, from house design to office building to art museum, indicated the architect's conviction of its multi-purpose potential. Mies was able to maintain this conviction, because the glass pavilion rested on subterranean spaces that could indeed accommodate many functions. In the case of the New National Gallery, the subterranean galleries abut a long open sculpture garden providing natural light from one side. Common spaces and offices remain largely without natural light. Furthermore, where light below is in short supply, it is generally provided too abundantly in the space above. The New National Gallery pavilion is at its best when left entirely empty, or used as a display space for large-scale, free-standing sculpture. Having built his first virtually program-free building in Barcelona almost exactly forty years earlier, the New National Gallery was for him merely a return of architecture to its natural terrain: a space constructed for the display of itself.

View of side entry stair, looking east, 1968

Model showing possible exhibition technique

Right:
Plan of pavilion (street level)

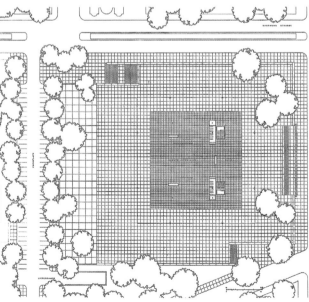

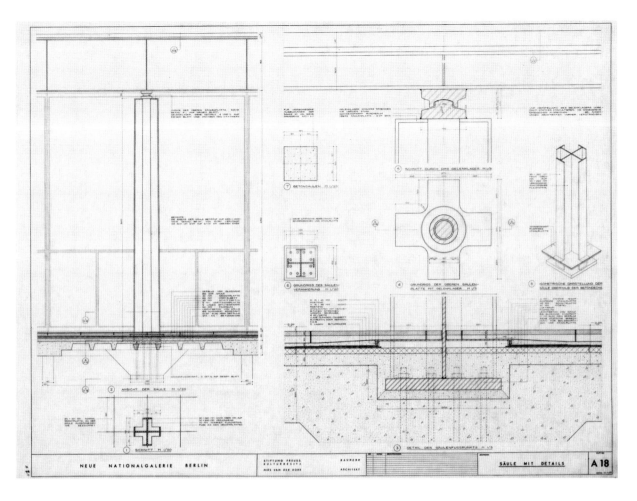

NEUE NATIONALGALERIE BERLIN

STIFTUNG PREUSS KULTURBESITZ
MIES VAN DER ROHE

BAUHERR
ARCHITEKT

SÄULE MIT DETAILS

A 18

Details of column-to-roof connection

Left:
Roof in the process of being raised by
hydraulic jack, late March / early April 1967.

1963–1969·Toronto Dominion Center
55 King Street West, Toronto, Ontario, Canada

View of banking hall with office tower behind

Following the successful completion of the Seagram Building, Mies began to extend the principles of its urban composition to larger assemblages of buildings, of which the Dominion Center constitutes an important example. Built in the 1960s, the complex dominates its downtown site. Other important examples of this form of large development include the Federal Center in Chicago (1959–1969) and the Westmount Center in Montreal (1964–1967), both projects also executed during the last decade of Mies's long life.

The Dominion Center continues the familiar theme of structures erected on a podium containing subterranean architecture, familiar since the beginning of Mies's career in the 1907 Riehl House. In this case, the underground shopping concourse connects to Toronto's system of subterranean passageways, providing access to public transportation, and housing retail stores that is conspicuously absent from the Dominion Center plinth. Instead, the public space between the Dominion Center's two immense black high rises (one notably taller than the other) is occupied by landscaping, sculpture, and outdoor seating. In warm weather it accommodates outdoor performance and spontaneous collective activities. To compensate for grade changes over the expanse of the site, steps were required along its southern and eastern edges, where the northern edge remains nearly level with the surrounding street. Two high-rise banking buildings, of 56 and 46 stories, and a large single-story banking pavilion occupy the full city block. The project thus combines themes developed both at the Seagram Building and in the New National Gallery, further reinforcing the architect's claim to the development of a universal language and a series of flexible building types.

1967 ▸ Mansion House Square and Office Tower

Not realized ▸ London, United Kingdom

View of model collaged into photograph of site

Two years before his death, Mies completed a design for an office tower to stand on a square in the City of London. The commission was offered to Mies by the London developer Peter Palumbo, with enthusiastic encouragement from Mies's British employee Peter Carter. Its specific difficulty lay in its siting, in the heart of old London, in proximity to Christopher Wren's and John Vanbrugh's Church of St. Stephen Walbrook (1672), George Dance's Mansion House (1739), and Edwin Lutyens's historicizing Midland Bank (1936). The project thus demanded that Mies accommodate his own urban vision to an existing assemblage of culturally important buildings. He could not, as in Toronto, Montreal, Chicago, and New York, withdraw his buildings into their own precinct divided from the city by a plinth or podium. Mansion House Square thus presented a new challenge for Miesian architecture, which perhaps explains Mies's willingness to take on a project whose design he finished in his eighty-first year, after a recent bout of bad health. The lease on the site would run until 1986; the architect knew that there was little chance that he would see the project in construction. Yet he produced a design for a rather modest 20 floor bronze-clad high rise after careful study on site and two years of work back in his office in Chicago.

While renderings of the square illustrate a form of urbanism that has now been familiar for some time, their radical mixture of old and new found many opponents at the time. The Prince of Wales began his campaign against modern architecture with the fight against construction of Mansion House Square in the mid-1980s. In 1985 the building application submitted by Peter Palumbo was rejected by the British Ministry for the Environment.

Life and work

1886 ▶ Maria Ludwig Michael Mies born March 27 in Aachen (Aix-la-Chapelle), youngest of five born to a family of stonemasons. His father is Michael Mies; his mother Amalie Mies née Rohe.

1896–1899 ▶ Mies attends the cathedral school of Aachen.

1899–1901 ▶ Mies attends the local trade school in Aachen and trains as a draftsman.

1901–1905 ▶ Holds various drafting jobs in Aachen.

1905 ▶ Mies moves to Berlin, where he works for the Rixdorf municipal department of building inspection as an ornamental architecture designer.

1906 ▶ Mies is employed at the office of Bruno Paul. *He receives his first independent commission: the Riehl House in Neubabelsberg.*

1907 ▶ *Riehl House commission completed.* Founding of the *German Werkbund*, an alliance of artists, architects, craft workers, writers, industrialists and businessmen. Among other founding members were also Peter Behrens and Bruno Paul.

1908 ▶ Mies goes to work for Peter Behrens, designer for the AEG (Allgemeine Elektrizitäts-Gesellschaft) and prominent member of the European architecture scene.

1910 ▶ Mies returns to Aachen, *competes for the Bismarck Monument with his brother, Ewald, (not realized) and designs the Perls House for Berlin-Zehlendorf.*

1911 ▶ Mies returns to Behrens's office, is sent to The Netherlands to work on Behrens's Kröller-Müller Villa.

1912 ▶ Mies leaves Behrens's employ when asked by the client to complete his own *design for Kröller-Müller Villa (unbuilt).*

1913 ▶ Mies establishes his own office in Berlin, and marries Ada Bruhn. *Werner House completed.*

1914 ▶ Daughter Dorothea born (in later years she would re-baptize herself "Georgia van der Rohe").

1915 ▶ Mies and family move to Am Karlsbad 24, subsequently his office, in Berlin-Tiergarten. Daughter Marianne born.

1915–1918 ▶ Military service in Germany and Rumania.

1917 ▶ *Urbig House completed.* Daughter Waltraut born.

1919 ▶ Rejected by Walter Gropius for the Exhibition of Unknown Architects in Berlin.

1921 ▶ *Competes in the Friedrichstrasse skyscraper competition with his entry, "Honeycomb."* Separates from his wife Ada and changes his name to Ludwig Mies van der Rohe.

1922 ▶ Mies joins the Novembergruppe. *Completes Glass Skyscraper design (unbuilt) for an unknown site, probably in Berlin. Feldmann House, Berlin-Grunewald completed.*

1923 ▶ Takes part in the exhibition of International Architecture, Weimar *Bauhaus. Completes Eichstädt House, Berlin-Nikolassee, Concrete Office Building project, and Concrete Country House project (both unbuilt).*

1923–1924 ▶ Contributes to and collaborates with filmmaker Hans Richter on *G. Material für elementare Gestaltung, later Zeitschrift für elementare Gestaltung.*

1924 ▶ Mies and other progressive architects found the progressive association of architects entitled The Ring. *Brick Country House design (unbuilt) for a Neubabelsberg site.* Mies orders his employee Sergius Ruegenberg to destroy office files and drawings of early projects.

1925 ▶ Meets Lilly Reich, interior designer, his companion and collaborator till 1938; receives assignment for "The Dwelling," the *German Werkbund* Exhibition at Stuttgart. *House for the painter Walter Dexel (unbuilt).*

Left page:
Mies at home in Chicago

Outing on the Havel, 17 May 1933, to mark the closing of the *Bauhaus*.
Mies (on the right) with daughter Georgia and "Bauhäusler" Fritz Schreiber

1926 ▸ Becomes vice-president of the *German Werkbund*. Karl Liebknecht and Rosa Luxemburg memorial at Friedrichsfelde cemetery in Berlin-Lichtenberg.

1927 ▸ "The Dwelling" opens in Stuttgart, with *Mies's Weissenhofsiedlung apartment block and other buildings, the Materials Show in downtown Stuttgart (with Mies's Glass Room), and an exhibition of architectural photography and models. Wolf House in Guben, Afrikanische Strasse Municipal Housing in Berlin.*

1928 ▸ Receives the commission to direct the German section of the Barcelona Universal Exposition. Obtains the commission for the Tugendhat House. *Completes addition to the Fuchs House (former Perls House) in Berlin-Zehlendorf. Bank and Office Building Project in Stuttgart (unbuilt).*

1929 ▸ Barcelona Universal Exhibition opens in late May (Mies' contribution: *German Pavilion, Exhibition halls for the industry, pavilion of the electrical industry*). *Completes Alexanderplatz Competition, house design for the painter Emil Nolde in Berlin-Dahlem, and Saul Adam*

Department Store design in Berlin-Mitte (all unbuilt).

1930 ▸ *Mies assumes directorship of the Dessau Bauhaus in August; Esters and Lange Houses in Krefeld are finished, and the Tugendhat House is completed in December. Mies places second in the Neue Wache War Memorial Competition, losing to Heinrich Tessenow. The Henke Addition is completed in Essen. Mies also completes drawings for an apartment remodeling for Philip Johnson in New York.*

1931 ▸ Mies receives membership in the Prussian Academy of Fine Arts. He directs and coordinates the Berlin Building Exhibition section entitled, "The Dwelling of Our Time."

1932 ▸ The *Bauhaus* moves to a factory building in Berlin-Steglitz. *Mies completes the Gericke House design (unbuilt).* "Modern Architecture: International Exhibition" opens at the Museum of Modern Art in New York.

1933 ▸ National Socialist assumption of power. *Mies completes Reichsbank Extension competition, and receives a prize. Completes Lemke*

House in Berlin-Hohenschönhausen. The *Bauhaus* closes due to reprisals of the Nazi authorities.

1934 ▸ *The Brussels Pavilion competition project completed. Mies is not awarded a prize.* He participates in the "Deutsches Volk—Deutsche Arbeit" exhibition in Berlin. Disbanding of the *German Werkbund* by the National Socialists (not until 1947 would the *Werkbund* be re-founded).

1935 ▸ *Mies completes the Hubbe House project for Magdeburg, a series of courtyard house studies probably intended to go with it, and the Ulrich Lange House for Krefeld. All remain unbuilt.*

1937 ▸ *Administration building for Vereinigte Seidenwebereien AG at Krefeld (unbuilt).* Mies visits the United States and Frank Lloyd Wright at Taliesin East. *Designs Resor House for Jackson Hole, Wyoming (unbuilt).*

1938 ▸ Returns to Berlin and leaves again, for permanent residence in the United States. Assumes directorship of the Armour Institute of Technology. Establishes Chicago Office.

1939 ▸ Mies begins master plan of Armour Institute of Technology.

1940 ▸ Meets Lora Marx, companion of his American years. Armour Institute of Technology renamed Illinois Institute of Technology (IIT).

1942 ▸ Designs for Museum for a Small City and Concert Hall completed (both unbuilt).

1943 ▸ Mies's first building, the Minerals and Metals Research Building, is completed at IIT. Design for Museum for a Small City completed.

1944 ▸ Mies becomes an American citizen.

1946 ▸ Alumni Memorial Hall (Navy Building) and Engineering Research Building completed at IIT.

1947 ▸ Perlstein Hall (Metallurgy and Chemical Engineering Building) and Wishnick Hall

Snapshot of Mies during a stay in Tessin (Switzerland), Fall 1933

1967 ► Westmount Square Development in Montreal, Canada, completed. Mansion House Square project in London, UK (unbuilt).

1968 ► New National Gallery completed in Berlin.

1969 ► Dominion Center in Toronto, Canada, completed. Mies dies 17 August in Chicago.

1974 ► Chicago Federal Center completed.

1986 ► Reconstruction of the Barcelona Pavilion completed (under the direction of the architects Cristian Cirici, Fernando Ramos and Ignasi de Solà-Morales).

(Chemistry Building) completed at IIT. Monographic exhibition of Mies's work at the Museum of Modern Art; exhibition installation designed by Mies.

1949 ► Promontory Apartment Building, Chicago, first project with Herbert Greenwald, completed.

1950 ► Cantor Drive-In Restaurant for Indianapolis, Indiana, completed (unbuilt).

1951 ► Farnsworth House, Plano, Illinois, completed; Lake Shore Drive Apartments, Chicago, another Greenwald development, also completed at the end of the year.

1952 ► The 50 x 50 House design completed (unbuilt).

1953 ► Mannheim National Theater design completed (unbuilt).

1954 ► Convention Hall design completed (unbuilt).

1956 ► Crown Hall at IIT completed.

1957 ► Mies is awarded with the medal and membership of the German society "Pour le mérite for science and arts". Commonwealth Promenade and Esplanade Apartments in Chicago completed.

1958 ► Design for Bacardí Office Building for Santiago, Cuba, completed (unbuilt). Seagram Building, New York, and Cullinan Hall, Museum of Fine Arts, Houston, Texas, completed. Pavilion Apartments and Townhouses at Lafayette Park, Detroit, Michigan, completed, Ludwig Hilberseimer, collaborator; Herbert Greenwald, developer.

1959 ► Retires from directorship of IIT and loses commission for campus buildings; developer Herbert Greenwald dies in a plane crash.

1961 ► Georg-Schäfer-Museum for Schweinfurt (unbuilt).

1963 ► Mies receives the Presidential Medal of Freedom from Lyndon B. Johnson. Lafayette Towers at Lafayette Park, Detroit, Michigan, completed, Ludwig Hilberseimer, collaborator.

America

USA
Chicago, Illinois
IIT Campus Master Plan
Crown Hall
Lake Shore Drive Apartment Buildings

Detroit, Michigan
Lafayette Park

New York, New York
Seagram Building

Plano, Illinois
Farnsworth House

Canada
Toronto, Ontario, Canada
Toronto Dominion Center